AF499305

# PAVING THE WAY OF THE DARKEST PERIOD OF INDIAN HISTORY AND REMEMBERING 21ST MARCH

VOLUME 2, ISSUE 1 OF BRAIN BOOSTER ARTICLES

MOHAMMAD AZHAD HASAN

# Contents

# Preface

"Start writing, no matter what. The water does not flow until the faucet is turned on".

-Louis L'Amour

Hundreds of students and professors are contributing their work to Brain Booster Articles, we are here to provide ample information about Law and Contemporary issues. Our aim is to provide a platform for today's generation to express their views and ideas on law and contemporary law.

# Publication

This research paper is published in volume 2, issue 1 of Brain Booster Articles

CHAPTER ONE

# ABSTRACT

The research paper consists of the detail of the reasons why national emergency was put up by the Indira Gandhi government in year 1975 and it`s consequences. The national emergency of 1975 was considered to be the darkest period of Indian democracy in which fundamental rights are suspended and people were put into jails and there was a gross violation human rights by organs of the government. It also has some positive affect on economy

CHAPTER TWO

# INTRODUCTION

In year 1975, Prime Minister Indira Gandhi declared an Emergency throughout the country. For the next 2 years, the Fundamental Rights of the people get suspended, several oppositions leaders get jailed and this part of the history is considered a black mark tarnishing Indian democracy.

But what were the exact reasons for declaring an Emergency? And why is it considered so terrifying? You must be surprised to know that 1975, was not the first time an emergency was declared in the country before this, during the 1962 Indo-China war and in1971 India- Pakistan war emergency was declared. Although the 1975 Emergency was different from other two, because it wasn`t due to war or any one reason.

CHAPTER THREE

# COMING BACK IN TIME

The sequence of events actually began in 1969, when the Congress party was in power and the Fourth Five Year was being implemented. In 1969 the Congress Party that, 14 private banks would be nationalized. It meant that Government would take ownership of those banks from the private companies. Several businessmen like J.R.D Tata, investors and shareholders opposed the decision of nationalism

On 18th July 1969, the government decided to pass it through an Ordinance, but soon the government realized that, the parliament session was due to begin on 21st July and the President was due to leave his office on the 20th, so, the ordinance was drafted in a hurry and almost overnight, it is signed by the President before the Parliament session began. You can clearly see how important this policy was considered by Indira Gandhi for the welfare of the country, the justification from Mrs. Gandhi that if these banks are nationalized then the banks could reach everywhere in the country and could provide their services even the poorest citizen that something for-profit company company may never do because think of there profit first. Basically it`s about socialism versus capitalism and their advantages and disadvantages. The bank shareholder will not be happy with their decision, there was a bank Central Bank of India and one of it`s shareholder was R.C Cooper, approached the Supreme Court regarding this decision and he earned a small victory in SupremeCourt. The court declared that the law enacted by the government, was discriminating against the 14 banks which were nationalized and that it was unfair to the shareholders, so, the ordinance by the government by the Supreme Court. Here begin the battles of the Indira Gandhi government versus courts.

CHAPTER FOUR

# BATTLE BETWEEN COURT AND THEN GOVERNMENT

When Supreme Court rejected the ordinance of the Indira Gandhi government, the government brought in anew amendment to the Constitution the next year and this amendment reverse the judgement of the Supreme Court decision. A few years later, there was similar case between Indira Gandhi government and Supreme Court regarding Privy Purse. Privy Purse is payment given to the royal families of the Princely States in India, it was practiced in India because when the government united all the Princely States to form India in 1947, then the condition was laid down that their ruling families would be given a payment by the Indian government. But Indira Gandhi did not like these payments, so, her government introduced a Bill to abolish Privy Purse, but this Bill couldn`t be passed in the Rajya Sabha that is why the government came up with new technique. They came out with a proclamation that the Princely States would ease to be recognized as such. It means that there would be no more ruling families in the country. Once again the matter reached the Supreme Court and Supreme Court declared this proclamation null and void. Then as usual Indira Gandhi government in 1971 added another Constitutional Amendment, that clearly stated that the Privy Purse would be abolished for the ruling families and the judgement of the Court was thus reversed. An interesting fact about is that the royal families protested this decision running elections. The Nawab of Pataudi at times was Mansoor Ali Khan Pataudi father of Bollywood actor Saif Ali Khan contested elections from Gurgaonbut only able to get 5% vote. But on the other hand, another royal family, VijayaRajeScindia and her son MadhavraoScindia contested elections and they won 1971 elections this is why Scindia family is involved in politics even today.

The battles between court and government were the reasons emergency was declared by the government. Coming in year 1971 this was the year when the Indira Gandhi won the elections again and this time becomes the dominant Prime Minister. Under her, centralization of power was evident and it is said that the Chief Ministers of the various states and the cabinet ministers, was being selected by Indira Gandhi based on who was favoured by her, an accusation that is being levied on the PrimeMinister Narendra Modi nowdays. Year 1971 was also they year when the India-Pakistan war took place due this there was a terrible effect on the Indian Economy, inflation rose and the prices of essentials commodities increased rapidly. At the same time Congress party had become so powerful that corruption had crept into it the Principal Secretary of Indira Gandhi had pointed it out himself. The corruption in the state government was worse. In 1974, the Chief Minister of Gujarat was Chimanbhai Patel a major scam involving him surfaced and people started calling him "ChimanChor" in Gujrat. People came out on road to protest, student protested, buses were burned, shops were looted and police was attacked. It is known as Navnirman Movement. This was a strong demand from the people of Gujrat to dissolve the state government. Indira Gandhi was left wit no choice so she dissolved the state government.

CHAPTER FIVE

# STATE OF ECONOMY

In 1973 there was terrible international oil crisis because of this by 1974, crude oil prices went up by 300% once again the common people suffered and inflation and price rise is seen. In the same year, a movement similar to the one in Gujrat began in Bihar by students it was led by J.P Narayan. Non-violent protests were held against the corruption of the congress government and the dissolution of the Bihar government is demanded. Another leader Jorge Fernandes carries out a 3 day long railway strike for demanding better working conditions and better salary for the railway workers more than 1.7 million workers protested in it and it become the largest industrial strike in the world at the time. “PURA RASHAN PURA KAAM WRNA HOGA CHAKKA JAAM” “JANTA KA DIL BOL RAHA HAIINDRA GANDHI KA SINGHASAN DOL RAHA HAI”. These were some of the slogans from that protest. A year has passed but Indira Gandhi did not soften like she dissolved the Gujrat Government because of the pressure, she doesn`t do in Bihar in fact, she claims that the movement were trying to end democracy calling them foreign funded anti-national movements but protest continue.

CHAPTER SIX

# FINAL ROAD TO EMERGENCY

Constant strikes, devastating inflation, price rise, unending protests and allegations for corruption. In March1975, Indira Gandhi gets another shock from Allahabad High Court. The thing was that for the previous 2 years there was case going on against Allahabad High Court this case was filed by the socialist election candidate Raj Narayan. He had contested the elections against the Indira Gandhi in 1971 from the same seat of Raibareilly in Uttar Pradesh. Raj Narayan was also an Indian Freedom Fighter but he is more popularly known for this case against Indira Gandhi. Raj Narayan accused Indira Gandhi directly that she won her election seat with unfair means and manipulated the ballots. 14 crimes were reported against Indira Gandhi but she was convicted only for 2 crimes by the court. The first crime was that she was using the UP government to build a huge stage to give her speech and second crime was that her election agent Yashpal Kapoor was a government employee even at the time of elections. Because of these court nullified Indira Gandhi seat of Lok Sabha seat as null and void and she was removed from Lok Sabha. Indra Gandhi moved to Supreme Courtto appeal this judgement. The opposition exploited this opportunity and they took to the roads to demand that the corrupt Prime Minister should resign. Morarji Desai said that a do or die movement was beginning against the congress. The decision of the Allahabad High Court had come on 12$^{th}$ June 1975, and what happened after 24$^{th}$ June was no less than a filmy drama. On that day, Indira Gandhi`s appeal was herd in the Supreme Court and the Judges said that all her privileges can be withdrawn that she may not be able to vote or contest election for next 6 years but she remain the Prime Minister till the next hearing. After the court`s statement, there was an uproar on the streets, the intensity of the protests of the opposition increased further.

Some congress leaders started protesting in favour of Indira Gandhi. The rallies against the Indira Gandhi on of those was led by J.P. Narayan he urged the students to come out and protest and stop obeying the police this is kind of Civil Disobedience and this will also be known as internal disturbance.

If we read Article 352 of the Indian Constitution it states that an Emergency can be declared by the President of India if India`s security is threatened by " war or external aggression or internal disturbance". Meaning that in India, an emergency can be declared for 3 reasons, the first reason is if India goes on a war with another country, second is external aggression and third reason is if there is a rebellion in the country. The last two emergency being declared in India, was because of the reason of war but this emergency of 1975 the internal emergency was used as a reason. On 25th June 1975, Indira Gandhi consulted with some of her ministers and on their advice sends a written note to the then President Fakhruddin Ali Ahmed, requesting that he declares an internal emergency in the country. And he does so, on the night of 25th June within few hours several opposition leaders were arrested including Morarji Desai, JP Narayan, LK Advani, and Charan Singh. The government cuts the power supply to the newspaper offices in Delhi that night so, that no newspaper could be printed the next day. The next morning, it is announced on the radio by Indira Gandhi of the emergency.

CHAPTER SEVEN

# CONCLUSION

So there were several root causes and reasons actually but the High Court judgement declaring Indira Gandhi seat to be null and void and the slogans of JP Narayan basically become trigger point because of which the emergency was declared.

What happened in the next two years is historic in itself this is known as darkest period of the Indian democracy, fundamental rights of the people was taken away and people continuing to protests were arrested. More than 1000000 innocent people were arrested, many oppositions leaders and activists go grounded during this period. Several organizations like RSS and Jamaat-e-Islami were banned even some congress leaders who were against the emergency were also arrested and was put into jail. Another scary thing at the time was the Mass Sterilization Program initiated by Indira Gandhi`s son Sanjay Gandhi to reduce the population of the country, the government sterilized some men forcefully in unsafe manner.

21st March 1977 emergency was called off and elections are held. Indira Gandhi and her son Sanjay Gandhi both lose their seats and Janta Party came into power for the first time. This was the first time that a party other than congress formed government in India. It`s another story that this government doesn`t last long and elections were held again in 1980 and in 1980, Indira Gandhi came into power again but this time around, her economic policies had changed a lot.

www.ingramcontent.com/pod-product-compliance
Ingram Content Group UK Ltd.
Pitfield, Milton Keynes, MK11 3LW, UK
UKHW021933200726
13853UKWH00010B/875

9 798886 410181